The Chicken Master

Chicken Akademy

Table of Contents

Recipes

CHICKEN TORTELLINI SOUP

ingredients

- × 2 carrots
- × 1 onion
- × 2 garlic cloves
- × 3 cans cream of chicken soup
- × 6 c. water
- × 1 tsp. oregano
- × 1 tsp. basil
- × 1 pkg. boneless chicken breasts, cut into bite-size pieces 1 bag cheese tortellini
- × 2 boxes frozen broccoli

directions

1. Cook the chicken in a small amount of oil.

2. While the meat is cooking, cut the vegetables and open the cans.

3. Add all of the above ingredients to a large pot, except the tortellini and frozen broccoli.

4. These 2 ingredients are added the last 10 minutes or so before serving so they don't overcook.

5. Simmer the other ingredients for an hour or as long as you like.

6. The soup tastes great with freshly grated Italian cheese and a loaf of Italian or French bread.

SEASONING MIX FOR CHICKEN

ingredients

- × 2 1/2 tsp. salt
- × 1 1/2 tsp. paprika
- × 1 tsp. onion powder
- × 3/4 tsp. savory
- × 1/4 tsp. coriander
- × 3/4 tsp. garlic powder
- × 1/2 tsp. black pepper
- × 1/2 tsp. thyme
- × 1/2 tsp. basil, dried crushed sweet

directions

1. Mix all ingredients well.
2. Makes 2 tablespoons plus 2 teaspoons.

MARINADE FOR CHICKEN

ingredients

- × 1/2 c. shoyu
- × 1/4 c. water
- × 1/3 c. salad oil
- × 2 tbsp. dried minced onion
- × 2 tbsp. sesame seeds
- × 1 tbsp. sugar
- × 1 tsp. ground ginger
- × 1/8 tsp. dried red pepper
- × 3/4 tsp. garlic powder

directions

1. Mix all the above ingredients.

2. Let the chicken parts marinate overnight, turning once or twice to make sure they are fully marinated.

3. Bake in 350-degree oven for 1 hour.

4. If you intend to use a charcoal grill, bake first in the oven for 45 minutes and on the grill for 15 minutes.

5. Place the marinade in a Ziploc bag with the chicken parts. This makes turning easier.

CHINESE CHICKEN SALAD DRESSING

ingredients

- × 2 tsp. sesame oil
- × 2 tbsp. sesame seeds, roasted
- × 2 tbsp. sugar
- × 2 tbsp. mayonnaise
- × 2 tbsp. lemon juice
- × 2 tbsp. oil
- × 2 tbsp. shoyu

directions

1. Combine all ingredients and mix well.

2. Drizzle over salad just before serving.

3. This is also a good marinade to pour over skinless chicken the night before grilling.

4. For the salad, make a green salad, with cooked shredded chicken.

5. Sprinkle the top with dry chow mein noodles.

CHICKEN CASSEROLE

ingredients

- × 6 chicken breasts
- × 2 onions
- × 8 c. water (approximately)
- × 3/4 loaf bread
- × Celery
- × Poultry seasoning
- × 2 tbsp.
- × Melted butter
- × 1 can cream of mushroom soup
- × 1 can cream of chicken soup
Sharp cheese, sliced

directions

1. Boil the chicken breasts with 1 onion in about 8 cups of water until tender.

2. Remove the skin and bones and separate them into pieces. Save the chicken broth.

3. Use a 13 x 9-inch pan (sprayed with Pam).

4. Cut small pieces of bread (about 3/4 of a loaf) and place them in the bottom of the pan.

5. Cut 1 onion finely and place it on top of the bread.

6. Sprinkle celery and poultry seasoning on top. Place the chicken pieces on top.

7. Melt the margarine and pour over the chicken pieces.

8. Combine the mushroom soup, cream of chicken, and pour on top.

9. Cover the top with sharp cheese sliced all over the top.

10. Bake until done.

CHICKEN POT PIE

ingredients

- × 3 lb. chicken
- × 1 can French onion soup
- × 1 lg. carrot
- × 1 lg. celery
- × Flour to thicken gravy Water
- × 1 double crust

directions

1. Preheat the oven to 400 degrees.

2. Simmer whole chicken in water with carrots and celery until done, 1 1/2 to 2 hours.

3. Remove the meat and cut it into small pieces. Refrigerate the chicken and broth separately overnight.

4. The next day, trim the fat from the broth, as well as the carrots and celery.

5. Add the onion soup and bring to a boil.

6. Thicken the sauce with flour paste and water.

7. Strain the sauce to remove the onions.

8. Put the chicken on the base of the base.

9. Pour the sauce on top.

10. Place the top base and bake at 400 degrees for 30 minutes.

CHICKEN WITH RICE

ingredients

- × 3 to 3 1/2 lbs. chicken, cut into serving pieces
- × 1/4 c. butter or margarine
- × 1 1/2 c. instant rice
- × 1 (10 1/2 oz.) can condensed cream of chicken soup
- × 1 c. water
- × 1 tsp. instant chicken bouillon crystals
- × or 1 chicken bouillon cube

directions

1. Preheat skillet (over medium heat) uncovered.
2. Add butter or margarine and let it melt.
3. Place the chicken pieces in a skillet and brown them on both sides.
4. Spice with salt and pepper.
5. Remove chicken from skillet.
6. Reduce heat to simmer "and add the rice.
7. Combine soup.

CHICKEN TIKKA

ingredients

- × 5/8 c. yogurt
- × 4 crushed garlic cloves
- × 1 1/2 inch fresh ginger, peeled & chopped
- × 1 sm. onion, grated
- × 1 1/2 tsp. chili powder
- × 1 tbsp. ground coriander
- × 1 tsp. salt
- × 4 chicken breasts, skinned & boned
- × 1 lg. onion, thinly sliced into rings
- × 2 lg. tomatoes, sliced
- × 2 tbsp. coriander leaves

directions

1. Combine the first 7 ingredients and set them aside.

2. Cut the chicken into 1-inch cubes.

3. Add to marinade, mix well, cover and chill for 6 hours or overnight.

4. Heat the broiler.

5. Place chicken on skewers or in a roasting pan and grill (or grill) for 5 to 8 minutes, turning occasionally until cooked through.

6. Garnish with onion rings, tomatoes, and coriander leaves and serve. 4 portions.

ITALIAN CHICKEN

ingredients

- × 2/3 c. flour
- × 1 tsp. salt
- × 1/2 c. vegetable oil
- × 1 green pepper
- × 1/2 tsp. pepper
- × 1/2 tsp. garlic salt Sliced onion
- × 1 lg. jar spaghetti sauce
- × Chicken (boneless) breasts, quartered

directions

1. Wash the chicken.
2. Mix the flour, salt, pepper, and garlic.
3. Cover the chicken, brown in oil, and then drain.
4. Top the chicken with bell peppers and onions (sliced).
5. Add sauce on top.
6. Cover and simmer for about 1 hour.
7. Serve with spaghetti.

LEMON – PARSLEY CHICKEN BREASTS

ingredients

- × 2 whole chicken breasts, boned & skinned
- × 1/3 c. white wine
- × 1/3 c. lemon juice
- × 2 cloves fresh minced garlic
- × 3 tbsp. breadcrumbs
- × 2 tbsp. olive oil
- × 1/4 c. parsley, fresh

directions

1. In a measuring cup, combine the wine, lemon juice, and garlic.

2. Pound each breast until 1/4-inch thick and lightly coat with breadcrumbs.

3. Heat the olive oil in a large skillet and brown the chicken, 5 minutes on each side.

4. Stir the wine mixture and pour over the chicken in a skillet.

5. Sprinkle with parsley and simmer for 5 minutes. Serve with the juices from the pan.

MARY'S CHICKEN DISH

ingredients

- × 6 pieces boneless breast of chicken
- × 4 tbsp. olive oil
- × 2 tbsp. butter
- × 1 clove garlic Breadcrumbs
- × 2 eggs
- × 1 bouillon cube
- × 1 can chicken broth
- × 6 slices of Mozzarella cheese

directions

1. Dip the boneless, skinless chicken breast in breadcrumbs and eggs.

2. In a large skillet, heat the olive oil, butter, garlic, and melt the bouillon cube.

3. Make sure to put the heat on low so the oil doesn't burn.

4. When the oil is hot, brown the chicken on both sides in oil, increase the heat so that the chicken is well and browned on both sides, lower the heat and add the chicken broth. Cook over low heat until hot.

5. Add mozzarella cheese to the top of the chicken.

QUICK CHICKEN

ingredients

- × 1 can cream of mushroom soup 1 can cream of chicken soup
- × 1 c. milk
- × 5 lbs.
- × Cut up cooked chicken 1 pt. sour cream
- × 1 pkg. Pepperidge Farm stuffing mix

directions

1. Mix soups, sour cream and milk.
2. Add chicken.
3. Mix all ingredients and layer in baking dish alternating with stuffing mix.
4. Bake at 350 degrees for 1 hour.

SWEET & SOUR CHICKEN

ingredients

- × 1 frying chicken
- × 1 tbsp.
- × Melted butter
- × Dash of salt,
- × pepper,
- × ginger
- × 3 celery stalks
- × 1 can pineapple (chunk)
- × 2 tbsp.
- × Brown sugar
- × 3 tbsp. water
- × 1 1/2 tbsp. soy sauce
- × 1 tbsp. vinegar
- × 1 tbsp. cornstarch
- × 1 red pepper (optional)

directions

1. Rinse chicken, place skin side up in oiled pan.

2. Pour melted butter over chicken.

3. Sprinkle chicken with salt, pepper, ginger, diced celery.

4. Bake chicken at 325 degrees for about 20 minutes.

5. Drain pineapple juice into cup.

6. Blend in brown sugar, water, soy sauce, vinegar, cornstarch.

7. Pour mixture over chicken in pan.

8. Top with pineapple chunks and pepper.

CHICKEN CACCIATORE

ingredients

- × 1 pkg. chicken
- × 1/4 c. butter
- × 1/2 c. sherry
- × 15 oz. can stewed tomato bits
- × 1 (6 oz.) can mushrooms
- × 1 pkg. Italian dressing mix
- × 1/4 c. chopped green pepper
- × 1 tsp. Italian seasoning Garlic powder,
- × to taste Bayleaf

directions

1. Boil the chicken until done. Save water (use this to boil rice).

2. Cut the chicken into tiny squares.

3. Brown in butter and sherry.

4. Add tomatoes, mushrooms, Italian dressing mix, green bell pepper, and other seasonings.

5. Bring to a boil and simmer for an hour. Serve over rice.

SUNDAY FRIED CHICKEN

ingredients

- × 1 whole chicken or any combo of chicken pieces
- × 1 to 2 c. of flour for coating
- × Salt and pepper to taste
- × 4 tbsp. butter
- × 4 tbsp. Crisco
- × 2 beaten eggs

directions

1. Wash and dry the chicken parts.
2. Combine the salt, pepper, and flour and coat the chicken.
3. Dip each piece in the egg mixture and brown each side in hot, melted shortening and butter. Lower the heat and cook for about 15 more minutes on each side.
4. Use a heavy iron or aluminum skillet if possible.
5. Remove from the pan and drain on a paper towel.
6. Pour all but 3 tablespoons of fat from the pan and reheat.
7. Add 3 tablespoons of flour to the skillet and stir with the fat until lightly browned.
8. Add 2 cups of milk and a little parsley or parsley flakes and cook over medium heat until thick.
9. Put in the sauce boat and serve with the chicken that has been arranged in a source.

HONEY BAKED CHICKEN

ingredients

- × 3 or 4 lbs. chicken, cut up
- × 1/2 c. margarine, melted
- × 1/2 c. honey
- × 1 tsp. salt
- × 1/4 c. prep. mustard
- × 1 tsp. curry

directions

1. Pour over chicken.

2. Bake at 350 degrees for 1 1/4 hours. Basting every 15 minutes.

BAKED CHICKEN

ingredients

- × 1/2 c. ketchup
- × 1/2 c. mayonnaise
- × 3 tbsp. minced onion
- × Bread crumbs or crushed corn flakes
- × 2 to 2 1/2 cut up chicken

directions

1. Mix the first three ingredients and dip the chicken in it. Cover with crumbs or flakes.

2. Bake in a greased skillet or lined skillet.

3. Bake at 375 degrees for 40 to 45 minutes.

SICILIAN CHICKEN

ingredients

- × 1 tbsp. plus 1 tbsp. saffron ace 1 lg. onion, sliced
- × 1 lg. green pepper, sliced
- × 1/2 c. fresh mushberries, sliced
- × 1 1/2 lbs. boneless chicken cubed
- × 18 oz. can tomato sauce
- × 16 oz. tomatoes, chopped drained
- × 1 tsp. Worcestershire sauce
- × 1 tsp. oregano
- × 1/2 tsp. basil
- × 1/4 tsp. garlic powder
- × Lite salt and pepper to taste

directions

1. Heat oil in large nonstick skillet.

2. Add the onion, green pepper, and mushrooms.

3. Cook until slightly tender.

4. Add the chicken.

5. Cook, turning chicken frequently until pink color disappears.

6. Add the remaining ingredients.

7. Cover and simmer for 5 to 10 minutes until heated through. Serve over rice.

8. Makes 4 servings (1 protein, 2 vegetables per serving).

ROAST CHICKEN WITH ALMONDS

ingredients

- × 10 chicken breast halves Salt and pepper
- × 1 (5 1/2 oz.) pkg. slivered almonds
- × 1 (10 1/2 oz.) can cream of mushroom soup
- × 1 (10 1/2 oz.) can cream of chicken soup
- × 1/4 to 1/2 c. dry white wine, or water or other liquid Parmesan cheese

directions

1. Spread chicken in a lightly greased baking dish.

2. Cover with

3. 2/3 of the almonds.

4. Mix soups with wine.

5. Pour over the chicken and almonds.

6. Sprinkle Parmesan cheese on top and then sprinkle with the remaining almonds.

7. Bake at 350 degrees for 2 hours uncovered. Serves 8-10.

WALDORF CHICKEN

ingredients

× 6 chicken breasts, boned and skinned 1 c. unsweetened apple juice

× 1/4 tsp. ground ginger 1 tbsp. cornstarch

× 2 c. unpared red apples, chopped 2 stalks celery, sliced

× 3 tbsp. raisins

× 1 tbsp. sliced green onion 1 tbsp. lemon juice

× 1/4 tsp. salt, opt.

× Ingredients: no

directions

1. Place chicken, 1/2 cup apple juice and lemon juice, salt, and pepper in a nonstick skillet.

2. Bring to a boil, cover, and simmer 20 minutes or until chicken is tender and cooked through.

3. Remove the chicken.

4. Mix in the remaining apple juice and cornstarch.

5. Stirring constantly.

6. Add the remaining ingredients. Place the chicken on a plate.

7. Top with sauce.

CORDON BLEU

ingredients

× 3 whole chicken breast, split, skinned and boned 3 slices (4 oz.) Swiss cheese, cut in half

× 3 slices (4 oz.) boiled ham, cut in half 2 tbsp. margarine

× 1 can cream of chicken soup 1/4 c. milk

× Chopped parsley

directions

1. Flatten the chicken breast.

2. Top each with 1/2 slice of cheese and then with ham.

3. Secure it with toothpicks. In a skillet, brown chicken chicken side down in margarine or butter.

4. Add the soup, milk and cover.

5. Cook over low heat for 20 minutes.

6. Stir occasionally.

7. Top with parsley.

8. For 6.

ORIENTAL CHICKEN

ingredients

× 1 chicken breast, quarter, cut into slivers

× 1/2 c. onion, sliced

× 1/2 c. carrots, sliced

× 1/2 c. mushrooms, sliced 1 tbsp. peanut oil

× 1 garlic clove

× 2 tbsp. low, sodium soy sauce

directions

1. Heat the oil in a large skillet or wok.

2. Sauté all ingredients except soy sauce over high heat.

3. Sauté for 13 minutes and lower the heat to medium and cook until the chicken is cooked through and the legs are tender and crisp about 10 minutes.

4. Mix with soy sauce.

CHICKEN YUM YUM!

ingredients

- × 1/2 pt. sour cream
- × 8 chicken breasts boned 8 slices ham
- × 1 can cream of chicken soup
- × 1 can cream of celery soup
- × 1 can cream of mushroom soup
- × 1/4 c. sherry cooking wine, opt.

directions

1. Chicken on the bone, wrap in a slice of ham.
2. Mix other ingredients together.
3. Place the chicken in a baking dish and pour the other ingredients on top.
4. Bake about 2 hours at 325 degrees.

CHICKEN IN ORANGE SAUCE

ingredients

- × 4 chicken breast halves
- × 1/4 c. flour
- × Salt and pepper
- × 4 tbsp. margarine
- × 1 1/2 c. orange juice

directions

1. Cover each half of the breast with seasoned flour.

2. Melt the margarine in a skillet and sauté each side over medium heat until lightly browned.

3. Add orange juice and cover.

4. Cook 15 to 20 more minutes over low heat until done.

5. Serve over rice, if desired, with the sauce. For 4 people.

CHICKEN AND RICE

ingredients

- × 3/4 c. rice
- × 2 cans cream of chicken soup
- × 1 pkg. Lipton cup soup cream of chicken
- × 2 c. water
- × Chicken pieces, about 2 lbs.

directions

1. Mix the rice, soups, and water and put in a greased 13 x 9 saucepan.

2. Place the chicken pieces on top and cover with aluminum foil.

3. Bake at 325 degrees for 90 minutes.

4. Remove the foil and let it brown for another 15 to 20 minutes.

5. It can be prepared the day before and refrigerated until baked.

CHICKEN PILAF

ingredients

× 1 1/3 c. Minute Rice

× 1 envelope onion soup mix

× 1 can cream of mushroom soup

× 1 1/2 c. boiling water

× 4 tbsp.

× Melted butter Sprinkle pepper and salt 4 pieces chicken

directions

1. Combine all ingredients in an ovenproof dish. Brush the chicken with melted butter and sprinkle with salt and pepper.

2. Place on top of the casserole mixture.

3. Cover with foil and bake 1 hour and 15 minutes until chicken is cooked. It can be arranged ahead of time and then baked.

POTTED CHICKEN WITH PEPPERS AND MUSHROOMS

ingredients

- × 4 chicken breasts
- × 3 green peppers
- × 2 (3 oz.) cans mushrooms
- × 1 lg. onion
- × 4 potatoes
- × 1 tsp. salt
- × 1/2 tsp. pepper
- × 1 1/2 tsp. paprika Oil for browning
- × 1 c. water

directions

1. Brown chicken and remove from pot; brown the sliced peppers and remove from the pot.

2. Brown the onions and mushrooms together; add bell peppers and chicken, as well as seasonings and water.

3. Cover and simmer after the first boil for 2 hours.

4. Remove the chicken, it should be soft.

5. Add coarsely peeled potatoes and cook an additional 15 to 20 minutes until cooked in sauce.

MARINATED CHICKEN

ingredients

- × 1 c. soy sauce
- × 1/3 c. lemon juice
- × 1/4 c. dry sherry or wine
- × 1/4 chopped green onion
- × 1 garlic clove
- × Pinch of pepper

directions

1. Combine all ingredients in a glass or ceramic container and mix well.

2. Marinate chicken for 12 to 24 hours then either grill or broil.

3. Makes enough for 4 to 6 pieces of chicken.

RUSSIAN CHICKEN

ingredients

- × 1 pkg. dry onion soup
- × 8 oz. bottle red Russian dressing
- × 8 oz. jar apricot preserves
- × Cut up chicken

directions

1. Place chicken in baking pan.
2. Combine ingredients and pour over chicken.
3. Bake at 350 degrees for 1 hour.

TURKEY DIVAN

ingredients

- × 1 (10 oz.) pkg. frozen broccoli
- × 4 lg. slices cooked turkey or chicken
- × 1 can cream of chicken or celery soup
- × 1/3 c. milk
- × 1/4 c. Parmesan grated cheese

directions

1. Cook and drain the broccoli. Arrange in a 10 x 6 x 2 baking dish.

2. Combine sour and milk.

3. Pour over turkey.

4. Sprinkle with cheese.

5. Bake in 425 degree oven for about 15 to 20 minutes until golden brown and bubbly. 3 or 4 servings.

SCALLOPED CHICKEN

ingredients

- × 1/2 loaf white bread cubed
- × 1 1/2 c. cracker crumbs, divided 3 c. chicken broth
- × 3 eggs, lightly beaten 1 tsp. salt
- × 3/4 c. diced celery
- × 2 tbsp. chopped onion
- × 3 c. cubed cooked chicken
- × 1 can (8 oz.) sliced mushrooms, drained 1 tbsp. butter or margarine

directions

1. In a bowl, combine the bread cubes and 1 cup of the cookie crumbs.

2. Add the broth, eggs, salt, celery, onion, chicken, and mushrooms.

3. Pour into a greased 2-quart casserole. In a saucepan, melt the butter, brown the rest of the cookie crumbs.

4. Sprinkle over the casserole.

5. Bake at 350 degrees for 1 hour. Yield: 6 to 8 servings.

CHICKEN A LA KING

ingredients

- × 1/4 c. chopped onion
- × 2 tbsp. chopped green pepper
- × 2 tbsp. margarine
- × 1 can cream of chicken soup
- × 1/2 c. milk
- × 1 1/2 c.
- × Cooked, cubed, chicken or turkey
- × 2 tbsp. diced pimiento
- × Dash red pepper

directions

1. Cook the onion and green pepper in butter until tender.

2. Add the soup and milk.

3. Add the chicken and the remaining ingredients.

4. Heat and serve over toast or cooked rice. For 4 people.

CHICKEN KABOBS

ingredients

- × 3 boneless chicken breasts
- × 2 jars baby juice (Apple or peach juice) Teriyaki sauce
- × Fresh garlic crushed One clove
- × 2 jars baby food peaches

directions

1. Combine the juice, peaches, garlic, and teriyaki sauce in a 13 x 9 plate.

2. Add enough teriyaki to your liking.

3. Cut the chicken into chunks to place on a skewer.

4. Put in marinade overnight.

5. Put the chicken on the skewers.

6. Cook on the grill. While cooking, drizzle well with marinade. Serve with vegetables over rice.

APRICOT CHICKEN

ingredients

× 3 - 4 lbs. chicken parts

× 1 (10 oz.) jar apricot preserves

× 1 (8 oz.) bottle Kraft Creamy French Dressing 1 pkg. Knorr's Onion Soup Mix

directions

1. Mix ingredients together and pour over chicken.

2. Bake at 350 degrees for 1 hour. Serve with rice.

BOWL OF THE WIFE OF KIT CARSON

ingredients

- × 4 c. chicken broth
- × 1 (15 oz.) can garbanzo beans, drained
- × 1 c. chicken, cubed and cooked
- × 1 - 2 chipotle peppers, minced, or 1 tsp. dried pepper flakes Dash Liquid Smoke
- × 1/2 tsp. paprika
- × 1/2 tsp. dried oregano, crushed
- × 1 med. avocado, sliced
- × 1 c. rice, cooked and hot
- × 1 c. monterey jack cheese, cubed

directions

1. Bring the broth to a boil; add beans, chicken, chili peppers, Liquid Smoke, paprika, and oregano.

2. Cover and simmer for 5 to 10 minutes.

3. Add avocado slices.

4. Place rice and cheese chunks in soup bowls.

5. Serve in hot soup. For 6.

CHICKEN A LA WORCESTERSHIRE WINE SAUCE

ingredients

- × 2 tbsp. veg. oil
- × 2 1/2 lb. chicken, cut up Salt and pepper, to taste
- × 16 baby carrots, peeled, or 2 lg. carrots, peeled and cubed
- × 1 med. red onion, sliced, or 16 pearl onions, peeled
- × 1 green bell pepper, sliced
- × 1 red bell pepper, sliced
- × 16 sm. mushrooms, sliced
- × 3/4 c. Lea and Perrins White Wine Worcestershire Sauce
- × 1/4 c. yogurt or light cream

directions

1. Heat oil in large skillet, season chicken, and brown pieces over moderately high heat until golden brown on all sides, about 15 minutes.

2. Add the vegetables and flip the glaze.

3. Drain off excess fat.

4. Pour white wine Worcestershire sauce over everything.

5. Cook 15 more minutes, basting occasionally, until chicken and vegetables are tender.

6. Add the yogurt or cream and warm. For 4 people.

BISCUIT DUMPLINGS

ingredients

× 1/4 c. Crisco

× 2 c. self-rising flour 1/3 c. milk

directions

1. Cut Crisco into flour then stir in milk. Drop by spoonfuls into broth.

2. Cover and simmer for 20 minutes.

CHICKEN AND BROCCOLI WITH RICE

ingredients

- × 1 1/2 c. water
- × 1 1/2 c. Minute Premium long grain rice
- × 1 lb. chicken breasts, boned and cut into strips 2 tbsp. oil
- × 1 (10 3/4 oz.) can cream of chicken soup 1/2 can milk
- × 2 tbsp. Dijon style mustard
- × 1/2 c. cheddar or Swiss cheese, grated 1 1/2 c. broccoli cuts
- × 2 tbsp. pimento, chopped (optional)

directions

1. Bring the water to a boil.

2. Add the rice.

3. Cover, remove from heat, let stand 5 minutes. Meanwhile, cook and stir chicken in hot oil until lightly browned.

4. Add the soup, milk, mustard and cheese, add the broccoli and bell pepper.

5. Bring to a boil. Reduce heat and simmer for 2 minutes.

6. Pour over the rice. For 4 people.

CHICKEN AND RICE ALMONDINE SQUASH

ingredients

- × 3 acorn squash, halved
- × 1/2 c. almonds, natural sliced
- × 1/4 c. margarine
- × 2 tbsp. maple syrup
- × 1 c. long grain rice
- × 1 c. chicken broth
- × 1/4 c. raisins
- × 2 tsp. orange peel
- × 2 chicken breasts, cubed
- × 2 tbsp. margarine Pepper
- × Garlic powder

directions

1. Bake squash at 350 degrees for 45 minutes in 1 water.

2. When squash is baked

CHICKEN BREASTS IN SOUR CREAM

ingredients

× 6 chicken breasts, split and boned

× 2 c. sour cream

× 1/4 c. lemon juice

× 2 tsp. salt

× 4 tsp. worcestershire sauce

× 3 tsp. garlic salt

× 1/2 tsp. paprika

× 1/2 tsp. pepper

× 1 c. breadcrumbs

× 1/2 c. margarine, melted

× 1/2 c. butter, melted

directions

1. Rinse the chicken breasts and pat dry. In a bowl, combine sour cream, lemon juice, and seasonings.

2. Roll the chicken breasts in the sour cream mixture, place in a bowl, and top with the remaining sour cream.

3. Cover; refrigerate overnight.

4. Remove the chicken breasts, absorbing as much of the sour cream mixture as possible.

5. Roll the chicken in breadcrumbs to coat well.

6. Place in a baking dish.

7. Mix margarine and butter; Pour half of the melted butter and margarine over the chicken and bake at 350 degrees for 45 minutes.

8. Pour the remaining butter sauce over the chicken and bake 5 more minutes. For 6.

CHICKEN IN SOUR CREAM GRAVY

ingredients

- × 2 sm. fryer chickens, cut up
Salt and pepper, to taste
- × 1/4 lb. butter or margarine
- × 3 c. milk
- × 2 tbsp. parsley, chopped
- × 1/4 c. sherry
- × 1 1/2 c. sour cream

directions

1. Season the chicken with salt and pepper.

2. Sauté in butter until golden brown.

3. Place the chicken and the fat in a saucepan.

4. Cover with milk.

5. Cook very slowly (around 325-350 degrees), around 30 minutes or until tender.

6. Add the parsley and sherry.

7. Cook for 5 to 10 more minutes.

8. Add the sour cream and stir into the sauce. Keep in the oven for another 5 minutes or more. Verify that it is ready.

CHICKEN BREASTS IN SOUR CREAM WITH MUSHROOMS

ingredients

× 4 whole chicken breasts, halved

× 1 (4 oz.) can sliced mushrooms, drained

× 1 can cream of mushroom soup

× 1/2 soup can sherry wine

× 1 c. sour cream

× Paprika

directions

1. Place the chicken in a shallow baking dish so the pieces do not overlap.

2. Cover with mushrooms.

3. Combine undiluted soup, sherry, and sour cream, mixing well.

4. Pour over chicken, covering completely. Sprinkle with paprika. Bake at 350 degrees for 1 1/2 hours. For 4 people.

CHICKEN AND DUMPLINGS

ingredients

- × 1 stewing chicken, cut into pieces
- × 4 c. water
- × 3 stalks celery with leaves, cut into chunks
- × 1 carrot, peeled and sliced
- × 1/2 c. onion, coarsely chopped
- × 2 tsp. salt
- × 1/4 tsp. pepper
- × 1/3 c. flour
- × 1 c. milk
- × 2 tsp. parsley, minced Biscuit dumplings (below)

directions

1. Combine the first seven ingredients in a large covered saucepan.

2. Bring to a boil. Reduce to a simmer for 2 1/2 hours.

3. Remove the chicken to a plate. Strain the broth, measure, and add enough water to make 3 cups of liquid.

4. Mix the flour and milk. Return the broth to the skillet and bring to a boil.

5. Add the flour and milk mixture.

6. Cook until thickened, stirring constantly, and simmer 3 to 5 minutes. Return chicken pieces to sauce and cover.

7. Make meatballs. Drop spoonfuls into a gently bubbling sauce.

8. Cover the skillet and cook for 20 to 25 minutes. Before serving, sprinkle with parsley.

CHICKEN BREAST WITH HONEY - WINE SAUCE

ingredients

- × 1 c. dry white wine
- × 4 tbsp. soy sauce
- × 1/4 tsp. garlic powder
- × 4 chicken breasts, skinned, boned and cut into pieces
- × 4 tbsp. veg. oil
- × 1/2 c. honey
- × 1/2 c. flour
- × 1 tsp. salt
- × 1/2 tsp. pepper

directions

1. In a large bowl, combine the wine, soy sauce, and garlic powder.

2. Add the chicken pieces, toss to coat, and marinate for 1 hour in the refrigerator.

3. Drain the chicken, reserving the marinade. On a shallow plate, mix the flour, salt, and pepper.

4. Lightly drain the chicken, one piece at a time, in the flour. In a large skillet, heat oil until moderately hot.

5. Add chicken and cook, turning, until golden brown on all sides.

6. Add honey to the reserved marinade and pour over the chicken.

7. Cover and simmer for about 15 to 20 minutes or until tender. Transfer chicken to serving platter and pour sauce over it. Serve over buttered noodles. For 4 people.

CHICKEN CASSEROLE

ingredients

- × 2 c. chicken, cooked and cut into small pieces
- × 1/4 lb. egg noodles
- × 1 can cream of chicken soup
- × 4 c. Stove Top Stuffing mix
- × 1 stick butter, melted
- × 1/2 c. milk
- × Butter 1 1/2-quart casserole dish.

directions

1. Cook the noodles according to the package, drain and pour onto a plate.

2. Top with cooked chicken and chicken soup.

3. Mix the butter with the filling mixture and put on top of the soup.

4. Pour the milk over the casserole.

5. Bake at 350 degrees for 25 minutes. Makes 4-6 servings.

CHICKEN CASSEROLE

ingredients

- × 1 (10 oz.) box Wheat Thins, crushed
- × 2 c. chicken, cooked and diced
- × 1 (15 oz.) can asparagus, cut spears
- × 1 (8 oz.) can water chestnuts, sliced
- × 2 cans cream of chicken soup
- × 1 c. Hellmann's mayonnaise
- × 1 c. cheddar cheese, grated 1 stick butter or margarine

directions

1. Combine soup and mayonnaise.

2. Place 1/2 of crushed Wheat Thins in the bottom of a 9 x 13" greased baking dish.

3. Place 1/2 of the soup and mayonnaise mixture

CHICKEN ALMOND CASSEROLE

ingredients

× 1 c. chicken breast, diced and cooked

× 1 can cream of chicken soup

× 1 c. sliced almonds

× 1/2 c. mayonnaise

× 1 c. celery, chopped

× 1/2 tsp. salt

× 1/2 tsp. pepper

× 1 tsp. lemon juice

× 3 eggs, hard-boiled

× 1 c. cracker crumbs (I use Zesta)

× 2 1/2 tsp. butter

directions

1. Mix in cookie crumbs and butter; set aside.

2. Combine chicken, chicken soup, almonds, mayo, celery, salt, pepper, eggs, and lemon juice. Grease a deep casserole and pour mixed ingredients in alternate layers with 3/4 cup buttered cookie crumbs.

3. Bake at 400 degrees for 20 to 30 minutes or until bubbly.

4. Top with remaining buttered crumbs and brown. For 6.

CHICKEN CHARDONNAY

ingredients

- × 2 (6 oz.) chicken breasts, boned and skinned
- × 2 tbsp. butter
- × 2 tbsp. shallots, chopped
- × 1 c. fresh mushrooms, sliced
- × 1/4 c. chardonnay (or other dry white wine)
- × 1 tbsp. lemon juice
- × Flour
- × 1 tbsp. veg. oil
- × 1/4 c. heavy cream Parsley, chopped

directions

1. Flat chicken pound; set aside. In butter, fry the shallots; add the mushrooms and sauté for 2 to 3 minutes.

2. Add the wine and lemon juice; simmer 6 to 7 minutes.

3. Dredge chicken in flour and season if desired.

4. Sauté in oil in a frying pan.

5. Add the cream to the mushroom mixture and heat until reduced. In hot plates, place the mushrooms on the chicken breasts.

6. Sprinkle with chopped parsley and serve immediately.

CHICKEN CURRY

ingredients

- × 10 chicken drumsticks (or other cuts)
- × 3 med. potatoes
- × 4 tbsp. curry powder (or more if desired)
- × 8 oz. sour cream
- × 2 lg.
- × Cooking onions
- × 2 piece fresh ginger
- × 3 cloves garlic
- × Salt to taste
- × 5 tbsp.
- × Cooking oil
- × 1 c. water"

directions

1. Cut the cooked onions, ginger, and garlic into smaller pieces.

2. Put them in a food processor and chop finely. Peel and cut the potatoes into quarters.

3. Mix the curry powder with a little water to make a paste.

4. Heat the oil in a nonstick Dutch oven.

5. Sauté the diced onion mixture until fragrant.

6. Add the curry paste and sauté, mixing well for 2 minutes.

7. Add the chicken and potatoes.

8. Mix well.

9. Cook, covered, for about 2 minutes.

10. Add sour cream and water.

11. Mix well.

12. Bring to a boil and reduce heat to simmer.

13. Cook, covered, over low heat for about 30 minutes.

14. Curry tastes best if it's made ahead of time and served later with warm fluffy rice or thick whole wheat bread.

CHICKEN ENCHILADAS

ingredients

- × 6 chicken breasts, halved, cooked and diced
- × 1 med. onion, chopped and saut√©ed in butter
- × 8 oz. cream cheese, softened
- × 1 sm. can green chilies, chopped
- × 1 pkg. med. flour tortillas
- × 1 can cream of chicken soup
- × 3/4 c. water
- × 8 oz. sour cream
- × Cheddar cheese, shredded

directions

1. Combine chicken, onion, cream cheese, and chili peppers.

2. Spoon into the flour tortilla and roll up.

3. Place in a greased Pyrex baking dish seam side down.

4. Combine soup, water, and sour cream.

5. Pour over the tortillas.

6. Bake in preheated 350 degree oven for 35 to 40 minutes.

7. Sprinkle with cheddar cheese and heat until melted. It can be served with rice and beans. It can be frozen, but omit the cheese before freezing. Serves 8-10.

CHICKEN PECAN QUICHE

ingredients

- × 1 c. flour
- × 1 1/2 c. sharp cheddar cheese, shredded
- × 3/4 c. chopped pecans
- × 1/2 tsp. salt
- × 1/4 tsp. coarse pepper
- × 1/3 c. veg. oil
- × 3 eggs, beaten
- × 8 oz. sour cream
- × 1/4 c. mayonnaise
- × 1/2 c. chicken broth
- × 2 c. chicken, cooked and cooled
- × 1/2 c. sharp cheddar cheese, shredded
- × 1/4 c. onion, minced
- × 1/4 tsp. dillweed
- × 1/4 c. pecans, chopped

directions

1. Combine the first five ingredients.
2. Add the oil and reserve 1/4 of the mixture.
3. Put the rest in the bottom of a cake tin 9.
4. Bake 10 minutes at 350 degrees.
5. Combine the rest of the ingredients and put them on the crust.
6. Sprinkle the remaining 1/4 of the mixture on top and bake at 325 degrees for 45 minutes.

CHICKEN SARONNO

ingredients

×   6 chicken breasts, boned, skinned and halved

×   Salt

×   Pepper

×   Garlic powder Curry powder Flour

×   1/4 c. butter or margarine

×   1/2 lb. fresh mushrooms, thickly sliced

×   1/4 c. Amaretto di Saronno

×   Grated rind and juice of 1 lemon

×   1 1/2 c. chicken broth

×   1 tbsp. cornstarch Patty shells

directions

1. Cut chicken into 1 wide strips.

2. Sprinkle with salt

CHICKEN WELLINGTON

ingredients

- × 4 chicken breasts, boned and halved
- × 1 pkg. Uncle Ben's Wild Rice Mix
- × 1 pkg. Pillsbury crescent rolls
- × 1 egg, separated

directions

1. Cook rice according to package directions. Beat the egg white and add to the rice.

2. Pour the rice over half the chicken.

3. Cover with the other half. Separate the dough into 4 pieces, using 2 rolls for each piece.

4. Roll each piece with a rolling pin until thin.

5. Wrap a thin piece of batter around the chicken, covering completely.

6. Place the chicken on a baking sheet and brush with egg yolk.

7. Cover the pan with aluminum foil.

8. Bake at 350 degrees for 30 minutes.

9. Uncover and bake for another 20 to 30 minutes until golden brown. Serve with currant sauce (below).

10. For 4 people.

CURRANT SAUCE

ingredients

- × 1 jar red currant jelly
- × 1 tsp. worcestershire sauce
- × 1 tsp. lemon juice
- × Dash tabasco
- × 1 tsp. dry mustard

directions

1. Mix together and heat over low heat until melted.

CHICKEN SHERRY

ingredients

- × 6 chicken breasts, boned
- × 3/4 c. olive oil
- × 1 stick butter or margarine
- × 1/4 bunch parsley
- × 1 onion, chopped
- × 2 c. beef consomm√©
- × 3/4 c. tomato juice
- × 1/2 c. dry sherry
- × 4 tbsp. flour

directions

1. Peel the breasts, roll them up and brown them in butter and olive oil.

2. Put the breasts in the toaster.

3. Add the flour to the oil and butter and add the remaining ingredients.

4. Cook a few minutes and pour over the chicken on the grill.

5. Cover the toaster and bake at 325-350 degrees for about 2 hours.

6. If frozen (sauce is best after freezing for a week), bake for just 1/2 hour.

7. Thaw all day when serving and bake for the remaining 1 1/2 hours at 325 degrees.

CHUNKY CHICKEN CASSEROLE

ingredients

× 4 chicken breasts, cooked and cut up

× 2 cans green beans

× 1 can water chestnuts, sliced

× 2 cans cream of chicken soup

× 1 c. mayonnaise

× 2 tbsp. lemon juice Cheddar cheese, grated

directions

1. Mix together soup, mayonnaise and lemon juice. In 9 x 13" pan

CONTINENTAL CHICKEN

ingredients

× 1 (2 1/4 oz.) pkg. dried beef, rinsed

× 3 - 4 chicken breasts, halved and boned

× 6 - 8 slices smoked, lean bacon

× 1 (10 3/4 oz.) can cream of mushroom soup

× 1/4 c. sour cream mixed with

× 1/4 c. flour

directions

1. Place the beef jerky in the bottom of a greased slow cooker.

2. Wrap each piece of chicken with a strip of bacon and place on top of the dried meat.

3. Mix the soup, sour cream, and flour.

4. Pour over the chicken.

5. Cover and simmer 7 to 9 hours (or high for 3 to 4 hours).

6. Serve over hot buttered noodles or with rice. Makes 6 to 8 servings.

CREAMY HAM AND CHICKEN MEDLEY

ingredients

- × 1 tbsp. butter
- × 1/2 c. fresh mushrooms, sliced 1/3 c. butter
- × 1/3 c. flour
- × 2 1/2 - 3 c. milk, divided 1 c. Half & Half
- × 1 c. parmesan cheese, freshly grated 1/2 tsp. salt
- × 1/4 tsp. black pepper 1/4 tsp. nutmeg
- × 2 c. chopped cooked chicken 2 c. chopped cooked ham
- × 2 (10 oz.) pkgs. frozen puff pastry shells, baked

directions

1. Melt 1 tablespoon of butter in large saucepan over medium heat; add mushrooms and cook until tender, stirring constantly.

2. Remove from the saucepan and reserve.

3. Melt 1/3 cup butter in saucepan over low heat; add flour, stirring until smooth.

4. Cook 1 minute, stirring constantly.

5. Gradually add 2 1/2 cups of milk; cook over medium heat, stirring constantly, until thickened and bubbly.

6. Add the whipped cream and the next five ingredients.

7. Cook, stirring constantly, until cheese is melted and mixture is smooth; add the chicken and ham.

8. Add enough remaining 1/2 cup milk for a finer consistency.

9. To serve, pour in the shells. The yield of the sauce is 10 shells. Note: This can be made a day in advance and refrigerated.

10. Either in the microwave or place on the stove to warm gently. It can be served over pasta.

11. Serve with a crunchy green salad.

EASY CHICKEN TETRAZZINI

ingredients

- × 1/2 pkg. fine noodles
- × 1 can mushroom soup
- × 1/4 sm. can parmesan cheese
- × 1 (4 oz.) can mushrooms, drained
- × 2 - 3 c. chicken, shredded
- × 1/2 pt. sour cream

directions

1. Boil noodles in salted water for 8 minutes.

2. Combine noodles, soup, cheese, mushrooms and chicken in a bowl.

3. Stir in sour cream.

4. Place in a greased baking dish and bake at 350 degrees for 30 minutes. Before serving, stir in a bit more cheese.

THE EYES OF TEXAS SAUSAGE CHICKEN CASSEROLE

ingredients

- × 2 c. chicken, cooked and diced
- × 1 lb. mild pork sausage
- × 1 c. celery, thinly sliced
- × 3 bunches green olives, sliced
- × 1/2 lb. fresh mushrooms, sliced (canned ones can be used)
- × 2 cloves garlic, finely minced
- × 2 cans cream of mushroom soup
- × 2 cans cream of chicken soup
- × 2 - 3 c. chicken broth
- × 1/2 c. wild rice, uncooked
- × 1 c. long grain rice, uncooked
- × 1 tbsp. worcestershire sauce (add to soup mixture)
- × 1/3 c. port wine (add to soup mixture)

directions

1. Cook long grain rice according to directions.
2. Cook wild rice about 45 minutes after washing well.
3. Drain both rices and mix.
4. Cook the sausage in a skillet until done; drain the fat.
5. Combine both soups and then add the chicken broth until you have a medium sauce.
6. Sauté the celery, garlic, onion and
7. Mushrooms until crisp-tender. In a large casserole, layer the rice, chicken, sausage, vegetables, and the soup mix.
8. Top with homemade bread croutons (see below) and bake at 350 degrees for about 45 minutes or until croutons are lightly browned and the casserole is bubbling around the edges.

FRAN'S CHICKEN

ingredients

- × 4 whole chicken breasts, skinned and boned
- × 2 cans cream of mushroom soup
- × 1 can milk
- × 16 oz. sour cream
- × 1 sm. bag Pepperidge Farm stuffing

directions

1. Prepare the filling according to the instructions on the package and let it cool.

2. Cook chicken, cut breasts in half and place in 9 x 13 "baking dish.

3. Mix soup

CHICKEN FRIED RICE

ingredients

- × 1 c. chicken, diced and cooked
- × 1 tbsp. soy sauce
- × 1 c. long grain rice, uncooked
- × 1/3 c. salad oil
- × 2 1/2 c. chicken broth
- × 2 1/2 c. onion, coarsely chopped
- × 1/4 c. green pepper, finely chopped
- × 1/4 c. celery, thinly sliced
- × 2 eggs, slightly beaten
- × 1 c. lettuce, finely shredded

directions

1. Combine the chicken, soy sauce, and 1/2 teaspoon of salt and let rest for 15 minutes.

2. Cook rice in hot oil in a skillet over medium heat until golden brown, stirring frequently. Reduce heat and add chicken with soy sauce and broth.

3. Cook over low heat, covered, for 20 to 25 minutes or until rice is tender.

4. Remove the lid for the last few minutes.

5. Add the onion, green bell pepper, and celery.

6. Cook, uncovered, over medium heat until liquid is absorbed. Push the rice mixture to the side of the pan and add the eggs.

7. Cook until almost done, then mix with the rice.

8. Add the lettuce and serve immediately.

Anatomy of the Chicken

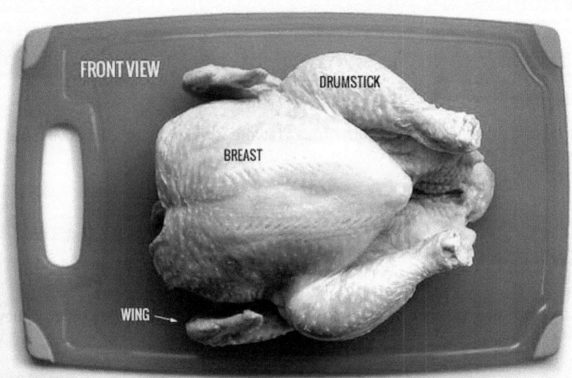

FRONT VIEW

DRUMSTICK

BREAST

WING →

SIDE VIEW

WING   THIGH

BACK VIEW

WING   DRUMSTICK

THIGH

ANATOMY OF THE CHICKEN

Head

The head is the talkie part of South Africa's famous walkie-talkies and stewing and braising are the best ways to cook it.

Breast

This very lean cut is best cooked quickly to keep them moist, for instance grilling, frying and braaiing. When stewing for braising breasts, don't overcook them as they will become dry and stringy.

Wing

Wings are high in fat and can withstand heat without becoming dry. They therefore are suited to deep- frying, braaiing and roasting. But however you cook them,

Tail

TAILS The tail is often attached to the thigh. It is packed with flavour because it contains a lot of fat and, thanks to the large skin area, becomes very crispy.

ANATOMY OF THE CHICKEN

Neck

This bony cut has very little meat but is an inexpensive way to flavour sauces and stock.

Thighs

Like drumsticks, thighs will be rather tough if not cooked properly. They have loads of fantastic flavour and are best when roasted or braised slowly or added to stews.

Drumstic

This popular cut could also be tough if it hasn't been cooked for long enough. The delicious dark brown meat particularly takes time and drumsticks taste best when they've been roasted, stewed, braised or braaied.

Feet

The other half of walkie-talkies, chicken feet are bony and low on meat. Once cooked, though, they are tender and can be eaten whole. Braai or grill them if you like crisp, crunchy skin.

HOW MANY CALORIES IN CHICKEN?

Chicken tenders

263 calories per 3.5 ounces (100 grams)

Back

137 calories per 3.5 ounces (100 grams)

Dark meat

125 calories per 3.5 ounces (100 grams)

Light meat

114 calories per 3.5 ounces (100 grams)

HOW MANY CALORIES IN CHICKEN?

Breast

A 3.5-ounce (100-gram) serving of chicken breast provides 165 calories, 31 grams of protein and 3.6 grams of fat.

Thigh

A 3.5-ounce (100-gram) serving of chicken thigh provides 209 calories, 26 grams of protein and 10.9 grams of fat.

Wing

Per 3.5 ounces (100 grams), chicken wings provide 203 calories, 30.5 grams of protein and 8.1 grams of fat.

Drumstick

Per 3.5 ounces (100 grams), chicken drumsticks have 172 calories, 28.3 grams of protein and 5.7 grams of fat.

Skin

While a skinless chicken breast is 284 calories with 80% protein and 20% fat, those numbers **dramatically** shift when you include the skin. One boneless, cooked chicken breast with skin (196 grams) contains: Calories: 386, Protein: 58.4 grams, Fat: 15.2 grams

COOKING METHODS

Grilling

This is one of the more common cooking methods, as it tends to require less added fat.

Baking or roasting

These other common methods are sufficient when you don't have access to a grill.

Broiling

This is similar to grilling, but you usually do it in a standard oven or toaster oven.

Braising

Lightly panfry the chicken and then cook it covered, submerged in liquid, for an extended time at a lower temperature.

COOKING METHODS

Fried

The chicken is submerged in hot cooking oil in either a pan or deep fryer. This creates a crisp outer coating but adds quite a bit of fat.

Baking or roasting

These other common methods are sufficient when you don't have access to a grill.

Boiling

You submerge the meat in boiling water and cook it until the internal temperature reaches 165°F (74°C). This is the leanest method, as it doesn't require added fats. Still, some may find the texture lacking.

Quick Recipes

Lemon Garlic Chicken

Place the whole roast chicken in the bakery with a whole lemon and a head of garlic (unpeeled) in the chicken cavity. Spice with salt and pepper. Cover with a lid and cook for 1-1 / 2 hours at 425 °. (Also try an orange).

Roasted Turkey Breast

Place the turkey breast in the bakery; Place 6-8 small red skinned potatoes, cut in half, around the turkey. Add 1/2 cup of white wine and 2 cloves of pressed garlic. Spice with salt and pepper. Cover with a lid. Bake at 350 ° F for 1-1 / 2 hours. Uncover for the last 15 to 20 minutes. Let stand 5 minutes before cutting.

Honey Mustard Chicken

Place the rotisserie chicken in the bakery and pour the fat-free honey mustard dressing on top. Cover with a lid. Roast 1-1 / 2 hours at 425 ° F.

3 CHEFS' TIPS
A little know-how can make life in the kitchen a lot easier

Done Yet

There are two ways to check if a chicken breast is done.
The first is to insert the tip of a small knife into the thickest part of the meat. If the juices run clear, it is cooked; if it's still pink,
you need to cook longer. Alternatively, make a small incision in the thickest part of the breast. If the meat is completely white and you don't see any pink meat, the brisket is done. The juices will also be clear. This method also works for testing whole chickens and other chicken pieces.

Slicing chicken breast for stir fry

Place the chicken breast, smooth side down, on a cutting board.
Cut diagonally into 1cm strips and cut each strip lengthwise in half into longer, thinner strips before cutting diagonally across the fibers to keep them tender.

Butterflying chicken breasts for schnitzels

Place the chicken breast smooth side down on a cutting board. Make a shallow incision along one side and continue as if you were trying to cut the breast into two identical halves. Stop just before cutting it all the way through, so the top and bottom half open like a book. With a meat mallet, tap the thickest part gently until it is finer and more uniform. Butterfly breasts can also be stuffed with any filling you like.

TIPS AND TRICKS

Keeping it Clean

×   Once chicken has been defrosted, do not refreeze it.

×   Don't let raw chicken come into contact with other food, cooked or un-cooked.

×   Always wash your hands, utensils and surfaces that have been in contact with raw chicken with hot, soapy water.

×   Keep a separate chopping board for raw meat to prevent cross-contamination.

×   Always make sure that meat is cooked through to kill all harmful bacteria that may have been lurking in it.

When buying chicken

Always look for chicken that has an even colour with no blemishes or bruises. The meat should look moist and plump and have a neutral smell. Check that the packaging hasn't been damaged in any way. When buying frozen chicken, make sure that the meat is frozen solid and does not have any soft areas where it has begun to defrost – and do remember to check the sell-by-date too.

Storing Chicken

Always refrigerate or freeze chicken as soon as possible after buying it. If the packet is damaged or soggy and you are going to cook it within two days, remove the chicken, pat it dry with kitchen paper and place on a plate. Cover with clingwrap or foil and put the plate on the bottom rack of the fridge. That way, it won't contaminate other food if it drips. If you want to freeze the chicken at home, remove it from the packet, pat it dry and reseal in an airtight bag.

TIPS AND TRICKS

Stop Breast Drying

How to stop the breast from drying out when MAKING roast chicken.
Roast the chicken breast-side down for two thirds of the cooking time. This way, all the juices will run down into the breast meat and keep it moist. Once you are ready to crisp the skin, carefully turn the chicken breast-side up and roast until golden.

How Tos and Hacks

Chicken salad. Place chicken breast side up on cutting board. Pull the
the leg and thigh away from the body and use your fingers to find the hip joint in the crease. Insert the tip of a large knife into the joint and cut through the skin, meat, and joint to separate the thigh and leg from the body. Repeat on the other side. Use the same method to separate the leg from the thigh and cut the wings from the body. To remove the chicken breast, cut the breast to divide the carcass in two. Cut all the bone and cartilage from the breasts.
You will now have two of each: thighs, drumsticks, wings, and breasts. Add the carcass to soups, stews or casseroles for flavor and remove the bones just before serving.

How to defrost a whole chicken

Thawing a frozen chicken is best done overnight in the fridge. Place it in a large bowl or on a plate to prevent the juices from dripping in the fridge. Before cooking it, check inside the cavity to see that there is no more ice. If pressed for time, put the bird in a bucket of cold water in the sink, but be sure to keep the water cold to prevent bacteria from growing.

TIPS AND TRICKS

Getting a golden skin

Check that the skin is completely dry, rub the whole bird generously with oil and season well.
Uncover the chicken 20-30 minutes before the end of the cooking time and place it on a shallow baking tray or on an oven rack on a tray to allow the dry heat to come into contact with as much skin as possible. Roast until the skin is crisp and glassy

Chicken and food poisoning

Raw chicken may contain natural bacteria, which could be dangerous if it hasn't been stored properly. Salmonella and campylobacter, which are linked to food poisoning and gastro, are among the most common.

3 DIPS FOR CHICKEN NUGGETS

Garlic and lemon mayo

Stir 2 finely chopped garlic cloves and zest and juice of 1/2 lemon into 1 cup (250 ml) Mayonnaise.

Tomato relish

Finely chop 3 small sherkins and 3 pickeled onions and stir into 3/4 cup (180ml) tomato sauce.

Sweet and sour

Stir together 3/4 cup (180 ml) pineapple juice, 1/4 cup (60 ml) apple cider vinegar, 1/4 cup (60 ml) brown sugar, 2 tbsp (30 ml) tomato cauce and 1 tbps (15 ml) cornflour. Thicker over a low heat.

Quick Recipes

Chicken Pot Pie

Simmer a couple of boneless, skinless chicken breasts, let cool and cube. Microwave cubed potatoes, carrots, celery, onion, green beans or peas. Combine with cornstarch-thickened chicken broth (from the simmered chicken), and pour into pie crust lined baker (you can use Pillsbury ready made) then top with the other crust, crimp, brush with milk, sprinkle with herbs, sesame seeds, or a little Parmesan, and bake at 350° about 40 min.

Cranberry Chicken

Mix one can of whole berry cranberries w/ can of cream of mushroom soup and one packet of onion soup mix. Pour over top of chicken in baker. Cover with lid, place in oven; bake for 1-1/2 hours at 425.

Chicken and Vegetables

Place chicken (skin on or off) in baker. Place chopped onion, celery and carrots around chicken. Sprinkle with 1/2 package of Good Seasons Italian Dressing mix. Place lid on top. Bake at 350° for 1 hour.

5 TIPS FOR GRILLED CHICKEN

Use bone in skin on chicken pieces

The thighs are highly recommended by grill experts, and I agree they are the most humid, but the legs, breasts, and wings also benefit when the bones and skin are left intact, as they help insulate the meat from overcooked and make it taste so much better.

(However, if you're committed to boneless, skinless chicken breasts, the techniques you practice with the remaining tips will help you master them with practice, too).

Pasture-raised chickens, especially those of traditional breeds, are not only tastier but also more sustainable than factory-farmed poultry, so look for them in your area at the farmer's market or local grocery store.

5 TIPS FOR GRILLED CHICKEN

Season chicken well with salt

Most people make their first mistake even before turning on the grill: they don't season the chicken enough.

Using your best quality kosher or sea salt, sprinkle all sides of the chicken pieces as if you were finely dusting them with powdered sugar.

Everyone loves marinated chicken, but dipping it into any sauce, even barbecue sauce, will bring you more cooking complications, not more flavor.

5 TIPS FOR GRILLED CHICKEN

Preheat your grill and flames under control

A diferencia de otros alimentos que responden bien al calor intenso, el pollo requiere un calor moderado o medio-alto (entre 350 F y 400 F).

Ya sea que use una parrilla de carbón o de gas, pruebe los patrones de calor colocando su palma abierta a unas 5 pulgadas por encima de la parrilla.

Si puede mantenerlo allí durante 5 segundos, está dentro del alcance.

También tenga en cuenta dónde el calor es menos intenso.

En caso de un brote, mueva inmediatamente el pollo a estas partes más frías de la parrilla para evitar que se queme.

5 TIPS FOR GRILLED CHICKEN

Brown chicken pieces skin side down

Always cook chicken skin side down first and plan to leave it there for the next 20 minutes or more, or until almost fully cooked.

Why? You'll end up with a crisp, beautifully browned skin (remember, isolate the meat), plus the chicken will cook evenly to the bone.

In general, it takes at least 30 minutes to cook bone-in chicken to this temperature, so try to cook it skin side down for three-quarters of the total cooking time (20 to 25 minutes) before turning. and finish it in the second. side.

5 TIPS FOR GRILLED CHICKEN

Use your grill as an oven

After placing the chicken pieces on the grill, cover.

Now your grill will radiate heat both up and down, which is exactly what your chicken needs to get fully cooked.

The lid also controls airflow and prevents the flames of a charcoal grill from getting out of control.

Fat dripping will likely cause breakouts, so monitor cooking and move chicken away from flames into cooler areas of the grill when necessary.

If you are not sure if the chicken is done, insert the tip of an instant read thermometer close to the bone or just cut in the center for a visual check.

The 5 Most Common Grilled Chicken Mistakes

Mistake n. 1
Not knowing the right cooking temperature for chicken

Mistake n. 2
Cooking too hot, lead to raw chicken too quickly

Mistake n. 3
Turn the chicken to the grill marks and get a blaze instead

Mistake n. 4
Finish with hard, dry chicken

Mistake n. 5
Grilled Chicken Sticks

The Great Chicken

USE SKIN-ON-BONE CHICKEN

The skin protects the meat from drying out and, along with the bone, adds a ton of flavor. Also, this method does not work with boneless, skinless chicken, which should be grilled quickly over high heat.

GET OUT OF THE COLD

Remove the chicken from the refrigerator and let it spread out at room temperature while the grill heats up. If the chicken is too cold when it hits the hot grill, the meat will tighten and become tough and may remain cold and raw near the bone even after the rest is well cooked.

MARINATE FOR EXTRA GOODNESS

You don't have to marinate, but if you do, you'll be rewarded with tastier meat. Marino at room temperature while the grill heats up. Enough time to season the meat (soaking chicken in sour marinades can make the consistency doughy). If you want to skip the marinade, sprinkle the chicken generously with kosher salt before letting it sit at room temperature.

MAKE SURE THE GRILL IS AT THE RIGHT TEMPERATURE

You want moderately high heat that registers 400 degrees on a built-in thermometer when the lid is closed. Turn the knobs on a gas grill between the highest and medium setting. On a charcoal grill, distribute the incinerated coals in an even layer. The coals are ready when you can hold your hand a thumb above the grill for 3 seconds before instinctively walking away.

PREPARE THE CHICKEN SKIN

Just before placing the chicken on the grill, wipe off the excess marinade, then pull the chicken skin over the meat to cover it as much as possible. If there is extra skin on the thighs (lucky!), Wrap it over the skinless parts. This will help the skin brown evenly and keep the meat more tender. Place the chicken on the hot grill with the skin side down.

DO NOT MOVE THE MEAT

Cover the grill, opening the top vents on a charcoal grill. In this first stage of cooking, you want the skin to turn a deep golden brown. When ready, it will naturally break free from the grill. If it starts to brown too quickly, lower the heat. If you try to flip it over and it clings to the grill, let it sit longer.

TASTE THE MEAT

After flipping the chicken, cook it skin side up until the meat is almost cooked if you are going to glaze it and if not, it is fully cooked. To test the doneness, slide a sharp kitchen knife close to the bone. It should slide in and out easily and the blade should be hot. Any juices that run out should be clear. If you have an accurate meat thermometer, meat close to the bone should register 160 degrees for bone-in breasts and 165 degrees for dark meat.

GLASS EVENLY AND FINISH

COOKING

If you are glazing the chicken with the sauce, brush the skin with a generous layer when the meat is almost cooked (155 degrees for the brisket; 160 for the legs). Turn it over and brush the other side. Continue glazing and brushing at a steady pace until the chicken has a coat of caramelized sauce.

WAIT FOR IT

When you take the chicken off the grill, you'll be drooling from its smoky scent. But resist the temptation to do it right away. Let the chicken rest on the uncovered tray for about five minutes before serving. This will make the meat juicier and let the glaze soak up its flavor.

USE SKIN-ON-BONE CHICKEN

The skin protects the meat from drying out and, along with the bone, adds a ton of flavor. Also, this method does not work with boneless, skinless chicken, which should be grilled quickly over high heat.

GET OUT OF THE COLD

Remove the chicken from the refrigerator and let it spread out at room temperature while the grill heats up. If the chicken is too cold when it hits the hot grill, the meat will tighten and become tough and may remain cold and raw near the bone even after the rest is well cooked.

MARINATE FOR EXTRA GOODNESS

You don't have to marinate, but if you do, you'll be rewarded with tastier meat. Marino at room temperature while the grill heats up. Enough time to season the meat (soaking chicken in sour marinades can make the consistency doughy). If you want to skip the marinade, sprinkle the chicken generously with kosher salt before letting it sit at room temperature.

MAKE SURE THE GRILL IS AT THE RIGHT TEMPERATURE

You want moderately high heat that registers 400 degrees on a built-in thermometer when the lid is closed. Turn the knobs on a gas grill between the highest and medium setting. On a charcoal grill, distribute the incinerated coals in an even layer. The coals are ready when you can hold your hand a thumb above the grill for 3 seconds before instinctively walking away.

PREPARE THE CHICKEN SKIN

Just before placing the chicken on the grill, wipe off the excess marinade, then pull the chicken skin over the meat to cover it as much as possible. If there is extra skin on the thighs (lucky!), Wrap it over the skinless parts. This will help the skin brown evenly and keep the meat more tender. Place the chicken on the hot grill with the skin side down.

DO NOT MOVE THE MEA

Cover the grill, opening the top vents on a charcoal grill. In this first stage of cooking, you want the skin to turn a deep golden brown. When ready, it will naturally break free from the grill. If it starts to brown too quickly, lower the heat. If you try to flip it over and it clings to the grill, let it sit longer.

TASTE THE MEAT

After flipping the chicken, cook it skin side up until the meat is almost cooked if you are going to glaze it and if not, it is fully cooked. To test the doneness, slide a sharp kitchen knife close to the bone. It should slide in and out easily and the blade should be hot. Any juices that run out should be clear. If you have an accurate meat thermometer, meat close to the bone should register 160 degrees for bone-in breasts and 165 degrees for dark meat.

GLASS EVENLY AND FINISH COOKING

If you are glazing the chicken with the sauce, brush the skin with a generous layer when the meat is almost cooked (155 degrees for the brisket; 160 for the legs). Turn it over and brush the other side. Continue glazing and brushing at a steady pace until the chicken has a coat of caramelized sauce.

Lightning Source UK Ltd.
Milton Keynes UK
UKHW050633110621
385329UK00002B/312